The Autobiography of a Broken Kid

Selected Poems & Flash Fiction
by Levi J. Mericle

Contents

The Desert Teddy

I grew up in the country
by the highway,
on Route 66.
And I stared day to day into the deserted pastures
of prickly teddy bears.
No grizzly, polar, or little brown
The kind that eats herring off a brook.
Yet I see charisma characterized
in these paws of shapened nature
These grizzlies of the desert,
these polars of the sand,
these little browns colored green

roar to the sound of existence.

Previously published in Outsider Poetry

Correspondence Hill

She wanted to climb with me up the hill on the side of a random road.
Darkness spat upon the sky like snuff in a bottle–

but still, we ran up the grassy plain.
We laid in the waves of weeds,
forgetting our curfew,
forgetting to remind each other of the trouble ahead.

We groped the sky with our eyes as if making love to the moon.
Chuckles of ignorant adolescent love made us forget that the car
was running.
Yet made us remember how we didn't care.
And I didn't care because her hand fit in mine like a baseball in a mitt.

Perfectly fitting as if meant to be held,
as if meant to win the world series.

I want to recite every word spoken that night.
Every awkward youth-filled pause of giggles that made our
conversations memorable.

I want to rekindle the bonfire in my heart
that singed my t-shirt with palpitations.
Because someday when we are old and dying,
I will remember that moment on the hill.

The moment I fell in love with loving you!

America

You fat and slothlike America
Clothed in Jewels and your Stepford Wives
You sit in camouflaged happiness
With millions, your billions
"Buy Me a pony, a condo"
"Give the poor a photo of what life is like,

Happy."

You slanderous sluts of gossip
Folded cackle for life's little gnomes of poverty
Fits of "give me more, you tired, you POOR"

You call yourself a god or goddess of wealth
But you have no dignity
Past what your wallet can provide
You pretend yourself a god
Because the one and only God will not claim you

So sit in your caged habitat of wealth and pride
And forget that a life exists beyond your Prada-skinned world
Face the truth

(Your highness)

You fat
You slothlike America

Previously published in Dead Snakes

Kong of the Cage

-For Harambe

Dreams are made of the streets not bound by human laws.
Streets of cane and pink petals of the Rubiaceae.
Where the trees stand larger than any man can climb.
Streets where beasts are known as pedestrians,
feeding and defending their families.

Streets of solitude, streets of pain. But these are comforting streets.
Streets that pave the houses of millions, along riverbanks and
mountainsides.

These are cameraless streets.
Streets that aren't sickened by the disease of man.
That aren't an artificial Africa,
barred by steel cages and the camouflaged sense of freedom.
Dreams are made of streets.

Streets we can walk and feel safe.
Where the capturing look in the human eye is only something we
see in our nightmares.

Streets should be the path walked toward home.

These are our streets.
These are our dreams.

(Dedicated to the 17 year old male gorilla shot at the Cincinnati zoo in May, 2016.)

Previously published in the University of Madrid's Journal, The Journal of Artistic Creation and Literary Research

Apartment 109

I never thought I'd be revealing this or even expressing his proof of life, but he's my brother and I can't live with this anymore. It all started ten years ago on a Friday around six o'clock at night.

I put one foot forward, pushed all the force of my back into my arms, and hit the baseball square on. With jaws dropped open, we both watched it sail through the air as it came down and landed near the abandoned houses on the next block.

We ran in the direction of the noise and I could see clearly that the third apartment complex window, on the right, had a large hole. Johnny made his way around the back of the building as I headed for the front door. I figured it was locked, but when I placed a hand on the knob and pushed slightly, it creaked and slowly opened. I walked into the living area and I noticed kids' clothing and jerseys were scattered all over the floor. There were baseball size holes in every window that I couldn't see from outside.

Every room was empty except for the one that I hadn't yet checked; I saw that the door was cracked open. I could barely see anything, but what I saw was so unlike the rest of the house. It was a bedroom perfectly neat and clean. A bunk bed was in the corner of the room, along with a desk and baseball memorabilia everywhere.

While being skeptical and slightly nervous, I turned around and began walking out of the room. I heard voices soft and faint, but growing louder as I turned. They were calling my name. The light above me began to flicker, then I saw it. Two names were written in plastic lettering on the wall, Johnny and Jimmy.

I went ballistic and screamed out for my brother. I ran as fast as I could down the hallway into the living room when the floors and walls began to rumble. I had a hold of the door frame as it felt like dozens of hands kept grasping at my ankles. The screaming grew louder. Chanting, screeching out: "Jimmy! Save us, Jimmy."

And I knew one of the voices was my brother's. I kept kicking and fighting until somehow I was released. I ran home as fast as I could.

My parents called the police and they searched that apartment thoroughly but couldn't find Johnny anywhere. It was days, weeks, months and now years since my parents had seen my brother. But I see his face every time I pass that building.

I see him screaming my name, begging me to rescue him through that bedroom window. And every window in that apartment has a different face.

It's been ten years since his alleged kidnapping. They now think he's dead, but I know the truth. He is very much alive, along with the other souls trapped inside apartment 109.

And I can't get him out.

Previously published in Flash Fiction Magazine

Inevitably My Own

I don't want to die.

But I don't want to live knowing
death will be my only accomplishment.

I merge from bedpost to bedpan and back.
My splintered thighs plead with the battle cries of
too much comfort.

I am the broken people,
you see at hospitals, asylums, the morgue.

Cradling their disability like a church pew, a crutch,
like their long-lost lover found.
Like a starved dog clutches his bone.

I am the definition of broken.
But, I want my scars to remember me.

Every curve of my body,
every wrinkle of my skin.
Untainted, virgin to pain.

I want my scars to wear me,
and always remember where I came from.

I don't want to live
if it means living without myself.
But I don't want to die

if knowing all I did was die.

Every moment,
every memory

I find myself closer to the end now.

Clouds are calling me home
and the rain pours harder and stronger.
My bones weigh me down.

Remember me not as a dead man.
But as a life worth dying.

a man in escape from himself...

Black Lives Splatter

WHAT, ARE, WE, THINKING?

These are four words I yell out to emphasize the validity of what I'm trying to say.

Such as the words supposed to be screamed out to the authorities like,

I can't breathe.
Or I'm selling CDs.
Or I'm a black child underneath this hoodie.

Can we as human beings honestly say that the color of one's skin has anything to do with the vibrancy

of one's heart.

All these bigoted remarks –
sparks of your putrid degradation and hatred on a nation,
that's a nation of colorful differences –
makes me think and believe that you really shouldn't be a part.

Because where's the art in spilling the blood of someone you believe to be different from yourself.

How do we justify this?

For centuries we've been treating minorities with the superiorities of a white train of thought.
Knots tied to make nooses on a branch of a tree as we snicker

and watch a colorful individual swing.

How fucking dare we?

The whips that striped the backs of slaves so millionaire massas can feel fulfilled.

How dare we?

The policemen's club and pepper spray that mocked the actions of the civil rights act –
by making a mockery of flesh and blood.

How dare we?

I want you to take a knife and run it across the palm of your hand and tell me that the black person sitting next to you bleeds differently.

How dare we?

This isn't about just listening to the police
but it's about the police being justified beyond what justifies a race.

It's as if our gun is pointed to the preference of skin color
more than a preface of a crime.

How dare we?

Time places a border between our differences, I know.
You may try to make yourself think and believe that we are much improved

And yes that's true.

But until you can look at the black man your daughter's about to marry
without your stomach churning,
you have no right telling me black lives matter.

Until you'll let your young white son date a little black girl in
middle school
don't you dare tell me we are different.

It has nothing to do with time,
it has nothing to do with "LIVES MATTER"
it has to do with you removing the bigoted sunglasses you've been
wearing.

Because when I walk outside I see a bright blue sky
and a pitchblack night,

I see a rainbow when it rains
And people living and breathing in our world.

Because black lives matter.

So can you just lower your weapon of hostility and recreate your
heart to listen with your eyes.

And don't scrutinize.

So until you can erase all the past from your mind
and see the lives right here,
right now as equals,

don't tell me we are different.

BECAUSE BLACK LIVES MATTER...

So,

Should we define the daylight from the darkness of night?
Because black lives splatter just as red as the white.

Previously published in Painters and Poets

Turn Around

His psychiatrist always told him his hallucinations were due to the traumatic loss of his mother as a child. The way she died was horrifying and was a potentially scarring event for anyone, especially a nine-year-old. He suggested for his mental well-being that he should start over and not look back. So, he visited his mother's grave, placed fresh flowers, and said goodbye.

Fredric fled from his current situation, from his family, his friends and he left the United States to travel to Italy. He left behind everything he knew to start fresh. He met a girl near Sicily who he connected with in almost every way. They rented an apartment together, bought a puppy, and were ultimately happy. And his hallucinations vanished.

It was a Friday at around noon. The mail was just delivered to their apartment complex; Gabriela walked in the door and handed it to Fredric. He took the stack of letters and began thumbing through. He looked through bill after bill until, in the middle of the mail, was a postcard from his home town. A piece of tape held a withered pink carnation petal in the left hand corner under the text. He began reading the familiar handwritten words as his heart began beating faster and harder.

"I missed you, baby, why did you leave me?
"I told you I would be with you always but you still left.
"Turn around Freddy, Mommy's right here!"

Previously published in Mystery Tribune & Zero Flash

Through the Hallway to Our Bones

I remember the tales told to me as a child.
Dark-room stories geared to frighten children into believing she
existed.

But I've always felt a connection to her.

Her name was a blank space,
an error in time,
A razor-sharp spoon used to dig up the skeletons in your mind's
back yard.

Her heart was an empty safe

supposed to hold the value of her value –
yet it held the empty tunes which were consuming her.

Mother World remembered her name yet rejected her soul.

She wasn't quite afraid enough to love,
but instead too scared to care.

She would hum the melodies of banished songs –
as if inviting the dead to visit her,
to dance in their bones with her and the moon
in the naked midnight hour.

They say that the dead will remember the moon
as a small bowl of light surrounded by sheer darkness.

And at certain moments at night, she will appear to take your pain.

I remember seeing her silhouette in the hallway as a child.
I wasn't sure if she was there to take me
or welcome me.

Frightened yet curious I called out her name.

"Mother?"

She didn't answer me at first, yet I questioned her name again.
A fragmented shadow of a hand crept across the wall –
as if reaching for me

As if wanting to embrace my acceptance.

The feeling of cold yet warm steel running through my veins.

Pricking every nerve,
Shaking every bone,
mesmerizing all sensations within my existence.

She was the name spoken around campfires to frighten the mind,
the nightmares that slipped through your daydreams.

Many were afraid to speak her name
Many were afraid to think of her at all.

But it was that night when I found her.

Where she found me.

It was through the hallway to her bones where I found
my meaning.

It was through the hallway to my bones where she found

Acceptance…

And nothing else really mattered after that.

Obituary in Space

I wish I could tell you that the world was well. But she was very sick. Specialists diagnosed her with acute humanity and gave her just six more months to live.

These were the hardest moments of her existence as she watched her children die by the millions. Her headaches caused tsunamis, her nausea started typhoons, and her immortal heartache drowned them all in her tears.

She was a dying earth. And humans became an extinguished race. She was a melanoma on the face of the galaxy, a cancer in the mind of space and time.

She will be missed forever.

Previously published in 101 Words

Not My Fault

It wasn't my fault.
It flowed out of me like rainwater.
like bolts of pain sharper than the colorful cracks in the sky

It wasn't my fault
that my spine was aligned with flowers
flowers with spines like loose spiders in a tea jar.

Like verbose roses in a biblical pattern of beauty
yet patterned like frozen moths in the wind.

It wasn't my fault
I dreamed of your sanity last night.
As you caught the teardrop of my crazy
and watched it dissipate in your palm like a snowdrop.

But I couldn't forget this
this laughter of our souls.
And in essence, I needed you like stone.
A strong formation that would overtake all the tides that rocked
these shores.

But still, it wasn't enough to uphold.
I'm but a frail petal now,
from a flower with no name and no beauty to claim.

This is what I've become
a commentator without an event.

But only to be recreated into something I've only dreamed of
becoming.

A person without fear.

Fear of questions never answered with inside my entity.
Fear of existing inside a maze of thistle I can never escape.
Fear of never overcoming a certain space of myself ever being
fulfilled.
To have this absent terror of always being hollow,
is slowly diminishing into a butterfly effect of fulfillment.

Every time you cry, I will weep with you.
Every time you stumble to fall no matter where,
I'll bridge my arms across the world for a smoother walk in this
lifetime.

I will always remember the smell of your sorrow.
But I'll never forget the fragrance of what makes you happy.

Saying Goodbye

Older men declare war. But it is youth that must fight and die.
-Herbert Hoover

Cast Iron tears are easy.

When you're young
when you're broken
when your heart is heavy.

When death licks your ambitions like a lollipop—
And you throw away your desire
like the wrapper of life.

What is the taste of grief?
Iron, confliction?
Cheap attention or compassion?

When you died—
I cradled the thought of your mini corpse.
I disregarded the stiff, firm look of your eyelids.
And tried to remember your smile.

Forever hates you.
The ending embraces your bones.

Someday—
I'll wonder why
roses cry the way they do

like pails of petals poured

over concrete.

Previously published in JACLR, Journal of Artistic Creation and Literary Research, The University of Madrid, Spain and Outsider Poetry

Pattern of Ruins

Tell my world to shut off the darkness like a night-switch, because I'm afraid of what lurks inside her.

Tell my world that she never kisses me good morning anymore; I feel like depression is eating my soul inside a blackened alley where shadows go to die.

Tell my world why I can't forget my enemies within this prison of conviction in my eyes. That when happiness comes to know me, I may never know it hits.

Tell my world I'm sorry, but I couldn't save her from the damnation she was promised.

And from the end she has always expected.

Previously published in 101 Words

A Miracle Mericle

-For my Nephew, Matthew Mericle

You were born biblically beautiful.
Biblically beautiful in the sense
you were a miracle.

A miracle in the sense that you shouldn't have been born.
Torn from your mother like an autopsy in reverse.
Torn from her belly like a sick Alien-reincarnated-movie-pre-
miere-joke

Covered in your mother's birthing jelly
I imagine you looked like a baby about to die.
A baby just visiting only for a few moments, just to later say goodbye.
I could see it in your mother's eyes.

In your father's hands.
The way they shook while holding you
as if holding his baby boy was something to fear.

But he feared you.
We all did.

Fear gripped our throats until we were unable to say your name.
But now your name is all I think about.
Your little hands that were too weak to grasp
your little legs too weak to kick.

I remember your eyes,

glassed over with silent plea for help.
But no help could amount to the help you needed.

Your eyes are now a Bible that never gets opened
that never gets read.
Although I now have faith that you are happy.

Biblically and beautifully dead you are,
a heavenly mark left on this world.

You were a miracle in the eyes of so many.
A star shining bright in our eyes to this day.

Shine on, little man,
shine on.

The Autobiography of A Broken Kid

What is love, if not passion?
Like poetry without inspiration.

I tried mopping the tears of yesteryear
just so I could wring it into a glass for you to drink.
So you would know my pain.

But pain is relative, you said.
Yet empathy should hold no bounds.
The cost of living is a pricey one,
when you don't know how to spend your days.

But lately, I've spent my life writing love sonnets.
Words like birds, fly off the pages and into your soul.
I try to write the kind of poetry that will kill you a little.

Kill the normal aspect of your daily routine.
Because, like all of us,
I want to leave a proverbial footprint on the sands of time.

But I am not memorable.
I have no great constructive features
outlining my face, to make you think I'm a great specimen of
humanity.
I have no riches, no monetary accolades which make me the next
Bill Gates.
I'm just a man trying to scratch my name on the tree of life.

I'm like a broken kid in the middle of the desert.

No money, no company,
No home.

It's just me, my notepad and my pen.

And before my ink dries up in the scorching heat
I want to write my biography.
I want to tell the world of my pain but how I overcame it.
How life will not serve you lemonade
unless you earn it.

I do not dream.
I do not cry.
And I do not want to live unless it's a life worth dying for.

So when you read about me a thousand years from now,
don't remember me as a great poet or a storyteller.
But instead remember me as just a kid.
Trying to find his way home in the dark.

Redemption

*How we remember, what we remember,
and why we remember form the most personal map of our
individuality.*

— Christina Baldwin

Forgive me Father, but I am not a dying age.

Not a lopsided heart cage you pretend to enter.
Where all you'll find here is barbed wire
the rotting stench of heartbreak-meat
a dusty eulogy that was never read.

But instead you'll find the polished gleam of another
the intoxicating embrace of a soulmate.
A masterpiece ending to the story written by the stars.

Forgive me Mother, but I am not a postdated check
or a reserved royalty.

a loveless egg-sack the hen abandoned
a token black hand you shake but know is dirtied
a chuckle in your frogged throat by the mere mention of my
affliction.

No, I am a welcomed tourist in the land of embrace.
A carpenter with sculpted words and enduring tools a mother
would be proud of.

Forgive me Brother, but I am not a cobblestone staircase.
an ancient walk-place you have to bear.
it's a troubled trod for you isn't it brother?
A beckoned, godless terrain your feet must endure
a callused journey you'll never want to take again.

But I am a pillow-cased yellow brick road.
a foundation, a pathway that will lead you home.

Forgive me Sister, but I am not a lost cause with a simple clause
a freckle nosed brother you cherished once in a daydream.
I was never par for your course.
Always coarse in a smoothened jester of compassion
hollowed in ways I never understood until now.

Forgiveness must be earned.

And I am not graphite in a lead-penciled world.
I will write my signature among every other on earth
in the book eternity will remember —
in a book eternity will read.

Previously Published in the HIV Here and Now Project and The Body

The Life Of Words

"A poem for Lynsey"

I write to captivate!

I write to set free, the captives held hostage within your mind.
As if these verbs and adjectives are just merely an objective,
to conceive beauty without any comparison.

They say that words can change a person's life.

It can ultimately tear you down to an even lower basement of Hell,
or build you up to a complete believable sky-scraping walk into the
heavens.

Words have a way of changing the outlook of one's inner appearance.
I write words, so they may live.
So they can breathe through the lungs of imagery and symbolistic
idolization.
I write words to crumble your sense of security,
while counteractively assembling a sense of protection.

I write to unwrite the written.
To contort the sense of safety within the parameters of meter.
I write as if making love on a piece of paper.
Tracing the curves of my mind and spilling them out onto the
canvas of creativity.
While caressing the embodiment of fantasy and truly becoming
one with ecstasy.

I write like I'm tomorrow's last breath.
I write as if mankind's fate is dangling from a string
and my pen is the blade that holds existence to a standstill.

To write is to breathe the breath of syntax.
To live in the element of words.
To inspire,
to compromise,
and to ultimately change the way we live with our thoughts.
Writing is what brings us closer to the reality of a fantasy.
Only achievable through the blood of our ink and the stains
creativity leaves behind.
Anything is possible my friend!
You just have to know where to bleed.

*Previously published in the University of Madrid's Journal,
The Journal of Artistic Creation and Literary Research and
Sick Lit Magazine*

Porcelain Rose

Have you ever seen a desert rose die?
Have you held the remnants in your hands
as the warm breeze carries the dust like ashes in the wind?

Can you just for a second easily pretend that I am that rose?
A deserted desert lifeline that is cut off from the rest of the world.
Left to shrivel without a solitary drop of care.

Some days I replicate the feeling of being a desert rose.
I understand her pain.
Her interpretation of her dehydrated corpse.
Lying lifeless, rigid and dried up in the desert sun.

Then I pretend to be a cactus.
Sharp-edged, arid humility,
integrity so hardened for the sake of survival.

An unsightly living organism.
Untouchable by the human hand.
Yet so fully alive.

Striving in a world where beauty is not allowed.
Rendered deceased at birth.

How could something so ugly,
so coarse in appearance, so unmistakably dead to the human eye
live for so long?

Is it some symbolical punch line to a bad joke
that I'm simply not getting?

Or is the ugly satirical point of the cactus,
merely a door that opens in death for death
to a place where life is pushed away.

So I live in the desert but I choose to be the rose.
Beauty, so predictably destined to die
yet is a death worthy of the life perceived.

Because I choose to be the rose,
Because I accept what ails me,
Because I am beauty,

I will prevail not just in this life but in the next.

Remembered in time as a porcelain teardrop
in a sea of fire.

Previously published in Outsider Poetry

Child Gone

Her whiskey knees
were always too drunk to hold up her body.

Her palms were a flight risk
jumping in surrender whenever she felt captured,

felt insecure.

Her elbows were never pointing to shadows that didn't exist
but just to the ones no one claims.

Her shoulder blades sharper than the tongues of serpents
easily colder than any iceberg you could imagine,
slabbed in the middle of her back like the titanic awaiting to
plummet.

I always hoped and believed she'd acquire normalcy.

But to her being normal was too underrated for her understanding.
She believed she was a nobody's nobody.

Just a slab of flesh living in an earthly meat counter,
waiting to be consumed inside the belly of time.

I hated to know her,
Because knowing her meant I cared way too much.

Knowing she was just a child gone wrong
and living in the skin,
of pure oblivion.

That's what I hated the most.

*Previously published in Mused (A Bella Online Publication)
and Dead Snakes*

To Sylvia

Life set you going with a pocket full of dreams
Yet your lining grew, filled with nightmares
And you fell to the element of death

The morning sang to you a lullaby
But then skipped the stepping stones of earth
And let you fold into the stream of wasted wishes
Melody forgotten

I found why life gave up on you
God jealous of your poetry
The devil envying your smile

I don't know where your nightmares grow now
Or if you have any more at all

Maybe you're plucking tulips
Inside gardens where winter never visits
Or maybe you're sitting in the darkness
Lapping up a mirage of happiness
You now Ms. Lady Lazarus

You have walked the paths of life
And felt sorrow among the world
Yet your path is paved and growing golden with dreams
Still on earth

Please don't forget why you existed
Because earth will always remember your smile

You've set the path we walk on
You are a goddess in your time
A heroine among the dead

You are the melody
And a pocket full of dreams
Your legacy will never be plucked

You are the tulips
The dreams
You are Lady Lazarus
You are Sylvia Plath

Previously published in Dead Snakes

The Clackernoose

"For Poe"

There stands in the depth of night
A reaper at my door
To depict a certain shadow light
To remind me of what's in store

My fractured soul is steady
To embrace what life enclosed
My pillow rests plump and ready
To accept what fate has chose

I snarl at the brink of midnight dew
In exchange for a rapid chill
Yet my mind can only think of you
When the sandman comes to kill

The clock strikes one as I hear the hum
Of the Clackernoose and his clan
For they will not come in the morning sun
Or when the stars caress the land

They are made of demons and wonder
Of discretion, damnation, and filth
They appear in the sound of thunder
Clapping laughter at our guilt

Built with bodies of children they've eaten
Of embryonic means

They swallow the treasures that suit them
And wear skin as clothing scenes

Their shrilling speech will grind the mind
Like the stones against a pier
And they bleed a certain scented sign
Indented in the atmosphere

They feed on the weak of heart
Heartache is their meal of choice
And once you scream they simply start
To catalog your voice

The door frame starts its shaking
My candle blows its flame
A hand started simply taking, taking
My identity from name

My withered words are so very few
As I simply plea to stay
But the Clackernoose comes straight on through
To dismember me from day

Now I have no existence
I'm but a tainted apple tree
Like Adam and Eve, repentance
Is not a choice for me

I offered a symbolic flag
Of no disclaiming truce
As I fell into the choking hands
Of my fateful Clakernoose

When I Was Young

When I was young
young people knew how to be heard.
Shredded jeans and Kool-Aid-stained T-shirts
sported us, acceptance.
Today, we bruise the face of time
in hopes to be noticed.
We collect a pension of happiness
through someone else's misery
and fold our hand because it was dealt with a pure one.
When I was young
old people were the coolest.
Shrewdest and crudest maybe
but cool.
Today we pack them inside homes
and neglect them.
When I was young
demons existed everywhere
along with angels to kill the fear.
God was on high not only because we needed him
but because we wanted him.
When I was young
a pocket of change could supply change in a homeless man's life.
When I was young
music had meaning.
It stirred emotions so deep in our souls,
we could tunnel from song to song and never want to emerge.
When I was young
I always wanted to visit the past,
and patch the holes left by our forefathers.

Redeem the broken and tear down the walls of agony.
When I was young
I wanted acceptance,
but accessed it in the wrong manner.
I pigeon-toed my way through a people's hearts,
hoping to be caged into acceptance.
When I was young
I needed a swift kick in the pants,
to remind me that pain is in everything we do.
When I was young
a chapter in a book took half an hour
but lasted a lifetime.

Previously published in Eunoia Review

Do You See Me

Do you see me?
Do you see this skin?

I am Hitler
I am the Ku Klux Klan
I am Neo-Nazi
I am fascism in its richest form.

I am a Gringo
a cracker
I'm albino born
I am white.

Privilege wrapped in a beautiful Caucasian package that should be
adorned.

But, I am ashamed.

I can hear the ancient screams in my head.
The whip lashes
the dead crying out to be alive again.

I feel their striped backs and the slats in the cage.
The unwritten pages of every black life that should be in our
history books.
But they aren't.

I feel it.

the eyes glaring
pleading to me their master
for a cup of water.
For a crust of bread.

I hear the pleas of a people that were silenced for so long and to
what end.
To what end.

I smell the fumes from the chambers that held the men, women,
and children
because of the star they wore on their sleeves.

Because they were a breed of vulgarity in the eyes of a man
who felt his superiority should reign.
I can feel their agony.

The bubbling in their lungs, the numbing sensation of death
entering their bodies.
Until they are a naked pile of flesh on the floor.

Right now I want no more to be white
then the people that carried a color, the white man spat upon.

From dusk till dawn for centuries I've been white.

I am the white group that burned crosses on the black lawns of
America.
I am the white racist shouting Dixie behind the rebel flag at the
battle of Gettysburg.

I am the Neo-Nazi driving a car through a crowd in
Charlottesville.

I am the white hand of a cop wannabe pointing a gun at Trayvon
Martin and pulling the trigger.

I am a dictator that spreads genocide over a whole race of
people.
I am that bitter taste of history that will never be erased.

I am a waste of human color.

However, I am ashamed not of the color of my skin
but what it has represented for centuries.
I am not ashamed of the color of my skin
but of the heritage attached.

Because when I close my eyes I see millions of dead bodies.
Beautiful people, every single one of them.
Every one of them deserved more than this white man standing on
their memory.
Saying I'm sorry.

It isn't much to offer
but these words are dedicated to every person that felt inferior
because a white man told them their skin color wasn't good
enough.

And right now, in my head,
no one could feel lower than I do.

Because I am a gringo,
a cracker,
I am albino born,
I am white.

I am Hitler
I am Jim Crow
I'm the Ku Klux Klan
I am Neo-Nazi

Do you see me?
Do you see this skin?

I am ashamed.

Previously published in Journal of Artistic Creation and Literary Research

Does Petulance Trump Precedence (A Letter to our President)

Dear dictator with the suicide hair, commentator to the world.
Diagram with the diaphragmed lips of another modern-day Caesar.

You have a longitude and latitude voice of direction
directing us to your version of the truth.

But there is a reason why serpents display their tongues like guns,
rifles fired to anyone who treads their territory.

And we are simply mice in your forked-tongued world.

Belittle or be eaten. Relinquish or retire the right to your honor.

But honor is what makes a man strong.
It's what bricks his home and mortars his family.
It's what stripes his flag and dots his stars.

It's the red of his blood, the white of his scars and the blue of his
bruises.
It's the memories of a nation with pride without prejudice he tries
to remember.

But you've built a wall, a wall of resentment toward your procla-
mation of policy.

And we the people, the mice, are dragged behind your diplomacy.
Dragged like a trophy carcass by the thread of our future.
Stumbling to get back up on our feet.

But walls can only stand for so long; mice always find a way to
get through.

We are a strong people
and will uphold the constitution of what made our country what it
is today.

A place where we are not distinguished as mice or serpents, but
as Americans.

We will not fold,
we will not falter

We will prevail.

America the powerful,
America the great,
America the proud and strong.

Youth

There was a time when I would try to forget you,
in my mind where I was immaturely and improperly raised.
I was the pupil in my head, in a school of no rules.
I was also the teacher, the principal
my mother, my father – my god.
Tearing book pages like flower petals.
"Comply I will" or "Comply I will not"
And as they fell to become nothing but forgotten memories in the dust,
I understood the bitter smell of fallen lilacs, watching them slip
away from beauty.
Yet I did nothing to try to revitalize what a true god created.
Decisions being deciphered by a child with a delusional sense of
being a man.
I could pray to my crucifix and receive redemption,
while burning my Jesus piece in a barrel of no regrets
and do all this with a pure mind and clear conscious.
I was able to break hearts and forgot the past where broken
hearts forget the misery.
I was a god, a teacher.
A preacher to audience of many (if many meant every personality
I portrayed)
I needed glory to make my existence justified, yet I glorified the
injustice of every person I hurt
around me.
I needed a jolt of power.
I needed to be in charge.
I needed to be God.

Previously Published in Cavalcade of Stars

A Bottle of Gin (A Lyric)

My mother always said to me, look to heaven and try not to sin
But I told my momma I'm sorry, but I sold my soul for a bottle of gin
As my father preaches from the pulpit, and my mom sings a gospel hymn
I sell my time for some vodka and lime and my soul for a bottle of gin

My daddy always said to me, I was a fool wearing human skin
He said in Heaven is where I started at, but in Hell is where I'll end
He said God he has a plan for me, but that plan is wearing thin
Because all he sees in the future is me, myself and a bottle of gin

My brother always prayed for me, when the sun was turning dim
Because midnight was my starlight hour, until the sun came up again
Sometimes he'd call and say come home, but I'd never tell him when
Because I had a date with Mr. Fate, and a bottle of my favorite gin

My sister always cried for me, She said I'd drown before I sink or swim
She said when I die and go to Hell, the heavens will weep within
So I sat my sister in a chair and wiped the tears off of her chin
I said Hell has already come for me in the shape of a bottle of gin

My wife she said she'd leave me; she packed her bags and said you win
She said I could only have her back, If I'd stop drinking myself in sin
But I said goodbye and I shut the door, and poured myself a glass of gin
And my wife drove off in my new truck and never looked back again

My daughter she can't talk quite yet, her name is Amber Lynn
Her eyes they burn just like Hell's fire, when I stare too deep in them
But when I kiss her small forehead, and tuck her gently in

I wish to god my soul's not sold, for a bottle of my favorite gin

So I play theses cards of life I'm dealt while smoking fire and
shooting thin
Because the devil he 'aint done with me and I sure as hell 'aint
done with him
So I spend my days in my heathen ways and sign my life with a
token pen
Tell my god I'm sorry but... I done sold my soul for a bottle of gin

Will You Miss Me When I'm Gone

I want to be the photograph
you keep in your underwear drawer.

And when you pull me out,
if you pull me out,
I want you to remember the dead lilacs that surround my headstone.

I want you to recall the raspberry scent on your toast
I brought you almost every morning.

The sidewalk stare I gave you,
every time you caught me in a lie.

But I want you foremost to remember the rose petals that lined
the hallway to our bed.

And I want you to fantasize wanting me again.

Because that's all I want to remember.

Everything else just hurts too bad.

Previously published in Dead Snakes

What Have We Become

-Dedicated to the victims at Pulse

I woke up to a dream this morning.
A reality better kept in my nightmares.

This poison that secretes from man's hands
makes me question our humanity.

What are we becoming?

There isn't a shadow we won't question anymore,
no one question left unanswered.

I would like to tell you the earth is safe.
And that we are welcome to roam this world as free men.
That security in man's actions is all we need.
But unfortunately, that's far from the truth.

What is our responsibility as humans if not to be humane?
Why should we fear human connection, when connection is all we
have?

Why should we be terrorized inside our schools,
Our movie theaters,
Our nightclubs?

Our mere recoil has become something I never thought would
happen.
We've barricaded ourselves around the fear of another man's actions.

What are we becoming?

We shouldn't be victimized because of who we are,
where we live
or who we love.

I'm sorry to tell you this is our reality.
But the real question is, what do we do next?

Take away the torch, and the darkness consumes us.
Yet feed the fire with fire and set our world ablaze.

So, I have no answers.
No inspiring thoughts to lift you up right now.

All I can do is bid you farewell and hope that humanity will
change.
Because hope right now is all we have.

I woke up to a dream this morning.
It was a reality better kept in my nightmares.

And I thought to myself,
what have we become?

A Chapel, A Chamber Pot (And a Simpleton)

I slept in the wake of what was paradise

A paradoxical implement of my nightmares

Sleeping,
yet not awaking from sleep
Not awaking
because sleep was never an option
Never truthful

The sun,
an equivocal master of paradoxes
Shines through like a newborn god
Expecting a life
yet given a life without humanity
Without the choice of being god,

Standing in the light of what deems to be pure.

The moon,
quite the seducing character
Starved by the thought of being full
Questioning the ways of humanity,
Given a path,
yet not a way out.
Swallowing darkness as a way of being gracious.

Two worlds and a nightmare.

Chapel, a chamber pot
And me

"Pass me a gun, a bullet and a cloth."

BANG...

Now isn't that unity?

The Coffin House

Your years were a kind blemish.
A velvet-lined box with a stucco exterior.
Your cigarette smile tinted the perfection of your happiness.

And every time I gave you my heart,
you would exhale inside my passion with the chemicals of your
regret.
When songs were sung like smokers cough to desperate lungs,
I figured the tone would escape from your eyes— and blossom
like a lotus tomb.
To where, recovering from recovery would be something like an
empty table.

You sit every meal, hungering for a new start—
for something that is palatable.
I can't remove the sin from your skin,
the ambush of your character and your mind,
is something you'll have to retrieve yourself.
I know the cost of existing is almost too unbearable for you.
But when the climb of day doesn't hurt you anymore—

You will rise from your coffin, close the lid and bury your pain.
Keep the ashes of your thoughts in an urn on your mantle

and remember your resurrection.

Previously published in W.I.S.H. Press and JACLR

Humanity in its Weakest Form

We are a closeted freedom—
An abandoned sense of security.

We sort our days on the shelves of fortitude—
with the memories we'll always try to forget.

When water flows over the brook of time
we'll remember nothing of fulfillment.
We'll know nothing of songs—
sung like ambient grass-blades whistling in the wind to the sound of
humanity slowly killing itself.
The texture of life is a gritty one.
A rough-scaled mistress that pretends to desire you.
A life without stones is never truly worth its weight in gold.

Yet there was always a point of break.
When the arched support beams of existence are saddled with the
echo of collapse,
we begin to question our stability.
That's when our sense of safety becomes—
a viable concern.

We wait out our days like termites,
either ready to destroy or be destroyed.
The human bond is becoming less of a requirement and more of a
chore.

The heavens turned her eyes from us
as we prepare to face damnation without a supporter.

Without a voice on our shoulder whispering, "You will make it, it'll
be okay!"

The question now is—
Can we withstand the somber silence in the crowd?
The brutal stubble of pride that roughens our sense of faith?
Can we pretend we are not human anymore?
Are we all just dummies moving our mouths to someone else's power?

Where is the justice in that?
The right for a jury is geared for a criminal—

Yet we are judged and executed according to someone else's terms.
We all breathe stale air that reminds us of home.
We all stare inside the same sky where our forefathers saw light-
ning bursts of war.

War that paid homage to our freedom,
while bleeding into the soil that unites us.
We all tuck our children into bed and pretend for their sake,
that monsters aren't creeping among them.
Our enemies prey on us like hyenas.
Because the color of our skin or who we choose to love isn't good
enough for them.
It just adds up to this.
We are slowly decaying on earth,
where our rights as humans were never really a priority.
Time moves like bubble gum. Exciting at first—
and then builds to an enormous amount of pressure.

Only to pop away like yesterday's news.

Previously published in the Journal of Artistic Creation and Literary
Research

When Balloons Pop

Life is a party we are all invited to. Each person is a balloon of a different shape and color. Some roam free to fly solo, but many fly in a crowd. Some rise to new heights while others remain in eyesight. But all balloons have one thing in common. They eventually pop.

I was born just like you; a balloon that rises yet succumbs to an inevitable death.

Essentially, isn't Earth one large balloon? Awaiting its day to pop from the galaxy and from existence?

When it happens, will we be remembered?

Or will the party of life simply stop?

Previously published in 101 Words

Ode to the Drunkard That Wanted Me

The anvil of your breath was pressed to my lips by force.
A link of chain, chain-length in size grouped your neck
with barely an inch to spare. Your body-grease-covered arm tattoo,
amused me ever so slightly. But I guess
a naked woman with a snake tattooed on her ass
could make any young boy laugh.
Your teeth rotted like a spoiled avocado, smelt spicy with the tinge
of vomit.
Your clothes drenched in sweat, cheap liquor and the willingness
to rape.
You fondled my sense of security,
gyrating your words in my direction.
Your erected smile followed me with every move I made.
And believe me I made very little, if any.
Your slightest touch made my teeth shiver.
Quivering like a mermaid on the end of a sailor's harpoon.
What was this dream I entered?
My first kiss, kissed by you, a drunkard.
You're nothing to me but an echo in my nightmares,
A gremlin in my sea of Gizmos,
A locket around the drowning neck of time.
In that moment, in this life and the next.
I didn't hate you and I still don't hate you.
Just the thought of you I hate to think.
But I know I must.
And I know I will.

Previously published in Black Heart Magazine

To the Grandmother Who Never Cared

My compassion for you is like a vodka-stained liver
Like a quivering litter of puppies that heard their mother die to the
stuttering sound of life
while pushing out the lightning bolt of birth.

And at night I unearthed the moon again just to watch her die
away a little more.
Like my compassion for you.

My compassion for you is like the sizzling bullets between our bones.
As strategical stones align the footnotes of my bed like a riverbed
of memories
I will not be remembering.

This December in my tone as cold
as the telephone you couldn't pick up to call me back.
You lacked the certain pentacle of devotion
like an ocean of family we should have been
but were not.

My heart still sunburnt by the thought of rays like happiness
a grandmother's love should excrete.

But these concrete grave markers mark the territory of our story,
grandson and grandmother.

So yes…

I shudder to think of us.

Yet there was never much to be thought of.
You are just a face my eyes visited once every decade or so.

And as the snow piled like the memories I wish we had,

I can gladly say I'm happy.

Happy that my compassion for you has quickly diminished.

Because I was just merely a storybook
                               –that you could never finish.

Previously published in Quail Bell Magazine

To the 25-Year-Old Bully Who Thinks God Hates Me Too (This One's For You)

Your hands remind me of Hitler's.
The way you parade around the office high-fiving your white,
heterosexual friends.
As if saluting a bunch of Neo-Nazi 5th graders at a playground.
You walk with a strut around the office
as if goosestepping is a form of masculinity people actually find
attractive.
Well I don't.
You claim god is on your side.
Yet your fists are like anvils when you place them on my desk
as if you're pressing down on my chest while you test the waters
of this pansexual parasite.
Trying to scare me into a submissive river of righteousness.
Yet I will not sink into your murky, cowardly waters.
I will not baptize myself into your false beliefs.
You see, I can smell the white supremacy on your breath.
And your homophobic tongue lashes out so often,
I can taste the leftover bits of flesh from the backs of others you
have beaten, in the air.
And when you walk into the room a haze of forgotten gays still
lingers in the atmosphere.
But I will not fear you.
Nor will I swallow your shotgun barrel fingertips
every time you point them in the direction of my lips to hush me,
in hopes the back of my head flies off.
No! I will not back down.
I will stand up for every homosexual, bisexual, transsexual and
lesbian soul you've ever trampled over. Stand up for those who

you served guns for eyes
and bullet-like stares for the main course.
Stand up for the ones you treated like subservient humans.
You with the delusion of wanting to rid the world of our kind.
As if we were a "kind" the world needs rid of.
As if, because we love a different way than you do-
you can justify your cruelty with the loyalty you have for the cause.
A cause you actually believe in, just because someone else is different.
Tell me, does your god believe in your cause?
Does your god justify your acts as biblically humane?
Because the Bible says God created us all in his image.
And I'm imagining God is waving a pride flag right now!
Sporting all the colors of the very rainbows he created
And I believe he is looking down on you like you look down on us.
But with the disgust you so rightly deserve.
Because I serve a God of color
I serve a God of differences.
I serve a God worthy of praise because he created us too in his image.
And if you believe
that image is a gay one,
then go ahead, hate on us all you like.
But my God is a happy God.
Happy with this pansexual man he created in his image.
And I am proud to say, I am his child.
So...
To the 25-year-old bully at work who thinks God hates me too.
Fuck you!
You and Hitler can enjoy the afterlife together.
High-fiving and saluting your death away.
But I am going to be with God when I die.
In his rainbow sky forever...

Previously published in Elephant Journal

Greatest Love Story Never Told (A Lyric)

She wanted more of me but I wanted all of her
And everything in between was nothing but a blur
My heart was bound in chains until I met a girl
And now everything makes sense, inside my world

I want to be with her until time grows old
It will be like the greatest love story never told
Her heart is in italics but my heart's written in bold
We could be like the greatest love story never told
I want to be the heat, when her world turns to cold
I want it to be like the greatest love story never told
And when the cost of love becomes like lost or sold
I still want to be in the greatest, love story never told

God granted me a gift, she's like an angel heaven sent
I told her that before, and she asked me what it meant
Her lips were like a blossom, the color of a crimson rose
Her hips reminded me of lightning clinging to her clothes
Her voice was a whisper of gold, the richest tone I suppose
I told her we could be like the greatest, love story never told

I want to be with her until time grows old
It will be like the greatest, love story never told
Her heart is in italics but my heart's written in bold
We could be like the greatest, love story never told

I want to be the heat, when her world turns to cold
I want it to be like the greatest, love story never told
And when the cost of love, becomes like lost or sold
I still want to be in the greatest, love story never told

I Simply Don't Care

I wish I could spoon with the heavens
Yet I have an immune intolerance to God
My heart is presented in journals of medicine,
As too small to calculate yet too large to discard

I was prescribed rainbows for my depression
And the Bible for my heathen ways
But with every doctor I saw or shrink I discarded
I collapsed further into the darkness that binds me

I live in the attic of my mind, I sleep in the closet of my soul
My heart's an empty faucet unable to flow with love
And still I seem to find comfort beyond the capacities of care
The devil mixes me a cocktail and I lift his skirt and drink
I laugh at each corpse incidentally mistaken for life
And pleasingly fill my cup with their tragedies

I sometimes wish for difference
Yet because I'm different I feel wanted
Because my soul is ugly I can tragically and wonderfully discard
the world as ugly

I live in the attic of my mind,
I sleep in the closet of my soul
And I simply do not care if my mold isn't molded like you.

Motives

(Dedicated to the shooting in North Carolina. 9/28/2016)

This poem is not written based on this true event

I want to tell you a story.
One that doesn't start with once-upon-a-timed sequence.
One that doesn't end with a happily ever aftermath.

It's 7:52 a.m.
Two children walk side by side into a public school.
One child is known by almost everybody.

The other one sometimes gets remembered.

One has a motive and both have a mission.

The boy on the left wants to just pass history without falling asleep.
He wants to watch the seconds fall from the clock
like the blue bullets from master chief's gun,
so he can go home to his real mission-

Halo.

The boy on the right has lost all hope in video games,
all hope in saving lives,
all hope in enjoyment.
All of his master chiefs have abandoned him.

He's left standing alone in the middle of the battlefield of life with no
one left to save.

No one left to save him.

He packs a backpack on his shoulder.
The holder of destruction, without repercussions –

because he'll go out the way he wants to.

He justifies justice with the injustices he's been served.
He swerves into the bathroom right before the bell rings.
His knees clanking like bolts in an old soup can.
His palms trying to grasp his father's Glock–

but keeps slipping as if he were grabbing a stick of butter.

Butterflies flutter in his stomach along with a hollowed hunger
because breakfast wasn't served to him that morning.
No kiss on the cheek and a pleasant ride with mom in a minivan.

He left for school with a mission as his mother was on a mission for
a needle.
His father on a mission for the next time slot in a federal prison –

He is the garbage pail child,
society has marked him because of who his family is.

He sticks a filled magazine in the handle
and cocks his piece.
He takes a deep breath and then a release.

What are we to do with that?
How are we to handle it?

A child loaded with hate is even scarier sometimes than the loaded
gun he or she is wielding.

The empty feeling that fills your soul with abandonment as a child whose brain is underdeveloped,

is like sending a newborn to kindergarten.

It's like putting a kindergartener behind the wheel of a car and saying, you need to drive yourself to school today.

We place principles in the hands of children who receive no principles at home,

no principles with their friends.

There's no stable routine in their psyche that tells them they are redeemable humans –

No matter their background, no matter their current situation

they have worth.

But once you pull that trigger,
once you swerve that knife,
once you detonate that device,

there is no going back –

Two boys walked into a school that day.
Both with a mission.

One with a motive.
Both never again walked out.

Previously published in Apricity Magazine

We are a university of one.
One blood. One mind.
We are mankind.
Our actions hold up our spine, our revelations make up our mind.
Our perseverance is our belly
Our guts and our glory
Our grandchildren will tell stories to their grandchildren
About how we fought and clawed our ways from the slavery that
enchained our endeavors
Our sisters and brothers fought for measures that surpassed the times.
The gut-wrenching crimes that placed us in chains,
The police man's nightsticks that knocked in our brains,
but our rights will remain

forever...

We did that.

We are the different who make a difference
We are the remembrance.

So let it be known.

That the haters threw the first stones
But what they didn't know is that the bones of yesteryear's
skeletons have healed
And if the past wants to call us a sacrilegious act against their
beliefs

Well then, let it be so.

We are the epitome of freedom
And let me just say this right now,

I count it a blessing and a privilege
To be a part of an "orphanage for the sacrilege"

Because we are home

And because we are home there is no reason to leave
America is that home
And there is no going back

God bless our America,
God bless our diversity!

Empathetic Ways of Disgust

Thought to me,
Is like slipping on the peel of a sandwich, or crust of banana.
A sketchy mountainside that you're daring yourself to leap off of
Braces over the eyes of jagged process: when processing comes easy.

I bite the tongue of satin-covered flowers, to understand the taste
of beauty.
But beauty's texture is a lot like eating a flower, quite arid and bitter

I think empathy is the master of guilt
and yet I think very little of you.
Because I walked in the trenches of your mind,
thought is something I now try to avoid.

Getting Even

You cradle your words
Like the suffocation of pansies
and wait to be executed.
Your fingers twitch as if death makes you nervous.
He snickers like a hyped hyena waiting to slaughter your loyalty.
Your shy movements make him believe he has you.
He goes in for the kill.
The condiments of a sociopath pool out the corners of his mouth.
You make your last move,
and to his surprise you crown his ass with satisfaction.

Checkmate!

The Freak

She sterilized her hands every time she touched me,
shiver her shoulders like tree branches
as if a spider was crawling up her trunk.

I tried to convince her that my skin does not secrete poisons,
that a single kiss won't turn her lips into a toad
or a solitary hug break her bones like a vise.

She was afraid of connection of interaction between vessels.
she believed all people were harsh and dirty no matter their
delicacy or purity.

She wasn't a virgin and that was her deepest and darkest regret.
At 25 she repulsed herself, not to mention was repulsed by me.

I hated her insecurities yet couldn't stop thinking about her.
For a reason I cannot explain, I couldn't live without her shivers,
her awkward shackled-glow that only I knew.

I didn't care if her touch was sacred, I just needed to be with her.
I needed her mental-quirkiness to make myself feel whole.
Because without her,

I was just a fragmented man.

Cosmos of the Mind

Stone within a mirror, within my prosthetic-eye
I see everything that's menial. No matter how small
or depth of seal, I peel back no matter how surreal,
                              like a foreskin to comply.
I hone this craft I set to space, hinged to what I try
to do. But like my ship's hull was made too tall
for me to skim the night. But still I try to apply

and hold onto what is true. It's for this reason why we die
in a sea of our regret. Just as stars live underneath the shawl,
doesn't mean we should forget. Because after all,
                              that would be a lie.
In transient as I pass the stars, I try not to rely
on time. Because up here the meteors start to brawl
in rhythm much like a rhyme. And still the comets cry

awhile and yet they miss each other's eyes,
in a subtle way but not too small.
And this is why exactly why, I love to death the death I die.
Because we are all bound to crash and fall,
                              beyond the crimson skies.

            All while inside,
                        the cosmos of our minds.

The Daughter of Home

"I SHALL ENDURE! I WILL ENDURE!" Excerpt from I Am Joaquin

                          - Rodolfo "Corky" Gonzales

"Make it so! Make it so…"

Those were the last words of a dying woman
who cared about nothing but giving to others
and supplying the best that she could give for her family

but for many years was given very little.
A woman whose hands had put in more time
than her boss's' grandfather clock that she polished daily.

Who scrubbed the white back in the white man's toilets
but was too dark of skin not to mention too dirty to sit upon.

A woman who was made to believe for many years that she couldn't
voice her opinion
because of the brown in her name and not to mention in her
complexion.

A woman who cooked and cleaned,
whose sweat caked the handkerchief that was wrapped around her
brow,
fingertips that bled and blistered in the washtub
and whose soles and arches ached with the pain of an inhumane
way of agony
for just for scraps from the rich man's table,
hand-me-downs from a country-club society
and from a bigoted way of thinking.

A woman whose pride was stronger than any other patriot
that stood underneath the colors of the red white and blue
yet had to bow behind the shadows of an American white-man
success.

America the beautiful. America the proud.
Home of the brave.

Home of the hands that sowed your earth and plowed your fields
Home of the hearts that broke and were re-broken for the sake of
integrity.
Home of the feet that walked your streets,
that bled on the doorsteps of our freedom for a future in prosperity.
Home of the silence from mouths of a minority for so many decades.
Home of past memories that we can't wash away with soap and
water,
that we can't scrub like a stain.
Home to everything you know but were unable to be a part of for so
many years.

Yes,
So many men, women and children lived and died before the ways
of America
Could be enjoyed by everyone.

You have always been the sons and daughters of our America
A child in this house we call home...

America the beautiful, America the proud.
America of the blood and bone.

The Gift

I would have liked to just cough in your presence,
But I was afraid it might have brought you unrequited death.

You punched the air every day
but not intentionally,
as if to knock out the germs before they entered your lungs.

I would have loved to love you in the traditional way.
Yet I was afraid a tight hug would crumble you,
Like our Aunt's coffee cake that you were too young to try.

Your fist fit in my hand much like a marble in my palm
and your coo much like a baby sparrow
was like a song barley sung but always heard.

We needed you to be here but you needed way more than we
could provide.

Justice is but a pale child awaiting the sun
and you were but a baby, born on the fringe of heaven waiting to
fully enter.
I hate to think of you,
because all I see are your eyes peering into mine with the hope
that they would one day be closed forever in a painless state of
dreaming.

I'm sorry your eyes found nightmares while living.
And I'm sorry that I couldn't have loved you more.

I would like to remember you as a child in the sun,
burning with a sense of desire

for a gift that you've been given,
for the gift that I have received.
Your eyes are now closed and you can dream forever.
That is the gift I would never take away.

My Right

4,832 Times.

Yes you heard me right.

Four-Thousand-Eight-Hundred and Thirty-Two Times!

I've never really counted but I imagine
this is an accurate amount of times you've hated me.
Amount of times you've looked at me with disgust in your eyes as
I walked by
and all I saw and all I see is a person uncomfortable with me.

Yes my nails are black
and my thoughts are dark but my heart is as pure as yours.
My tongue's bones break every night
screaming out the words,

"WHY, WHY WON'T YOU ACCEPT ME?"

I don't understand it, I can't comprehend it
this hate you have for me is unbelievably strong
and I don't know what I did wrong.
I go to my bed every single night and cry my eyes out, until they
bleed,
until they bleed with a ghost of memories of me and I see nothing,
nothing but pure night.

And you wonder why I am so dark,
why I hide only one tiny little spark within my stare

and I only pull it out for those who care,
it's this facade I wear, I wear it like a crown of thorns
my God adorned for Calvary's chair.

But damn it why, why hate me, just because I'm different?

I still bleed pain like you, I walk, I talk, I think, I chew.
I am human too no matter what my views are like
or to whom I pray at night.
What gives you the right to hate me?

I am no hypocrite, I wear this shit on my sleeves
like the scars you can see
I am who I say I am now here's your chance to believe.
I am me.

I am not changing my look or rearranging my life.
I pray to the same god you pray to at night.
But unlike you I fight, I fight it every day of my life for the right to
ignite my spark,
So that you can hear me,
so that the world can see me inside the dark.

Yes this world is so cold like the shoulder you turn to spite me,
as the windows always see the lightning
and I see every bolt of hate you strike me with.

But let me tell you something,
my face is now uncovered
my eye sockets have now recovered,
these bullets have now resurfaced from this target which is my heart.

My wounds have healed my scars are sealed and I can feel,

no matter how many feelings you try to kill.
I am real.

Yes it's now been 4,833 times
you've committed these crimes but they don't faze me anymore.

Your hate is just a door that's opened and I'm closing it.

Because I am me
and I have the right to be me,
yes I have the right to be free.

And I am free!

Existence

My existence doesn't matter
I'm just a piece of glass like you
I scratch,
I chip,
I shatter
And I'm transparent through and through

My life it has no meaning
I'm but a stone in the river bed
My soul is cold and clammy
And I have a heaviness in my head

My heart it has no feeling
I feel nothing other than pain
My insanity's so revealing
I'm but an awkward social stain

My world exists of razor blades
Of knives and drugs and glass
My dreams withhold a pot of gold
Yet I'm a tarnished piece of brass

I do not have a heaven here
With robes of silver sash
And I can't even go to hell my dear
Because all that is left is ash

My pride is still not glorified
And I don't say what isn't true
I still scratch
and chip
and shatter
I'm still just a piece of glass like you

I Forgive You

Tranquility some say is what ashes are made of.

As these burning bones are smoldering inside the closets within
my eyes,
I remember his drunken smile.

His wasted reflection like a god is mirrored in my sledge-ham-
mered remembrance.

Nothing can take away from the past if the matches are never lit.
Nothing can burn if the spark isn't there or if the need isn't bright.

Nothing wholesome is pure.

I wish I could umbrella the thought of his face,
so he'll drip from my mind like raindrops in the summertime.

But these skies won't stop their bleeding.

The clouds won't quit their forming
and if heaven ever existed, I'm sure I would never know.

I was born when I was five.
And certain pieces of me died ten minutes later,
when he entered the door and into my life.

Together we made the most tragic memory.
Iconic in a way a child should never experience.

I'll never forget his mystifying yet rape-like stare that captivated
my soul in all the wrong ways.

I never meant for him to leave this imprint.
And I'm sure, if he were still alive, he wouldn't have remembered
me at all.
Or remember when I was growing up, I feared entering a Men's
restroom.

I was terrified being alone with any man to the point, I couldn't
even see a doctor,
without my blood boiling.

PTSD-moments of his body type, his words and his smell left an
indention so deep,
that to this day it's hard to hammer out.

Although I can never forget, I'll never forgive myself for not
forgiving him.

Because ashes are meant to be swept away.
The bones in my closet's eye are merely dust now.
To the man whose face echoed in my mind ever since I was a child

I forgive you.

Previously published in PenHead Press

It's Almost Her

"She's just a piece of paper, that's folded in a crease.
You want the demons out of her, then go call a fucking priest."

It's almost childlike,
the way she balls her fist to rub her eyes when she's tired.
The way when she cries, her bottom lip protrudes about an inch
away from her face.
And the way she looks at me when we're having sex, makes me
feel dirty all over.

It's almost disturbing,
the way she grips her dinner fork at mealtime.
As if the pile of steamed and flavored pork were her victim
waiting to be prodded.

It's almost disgusting,
the way she portrays dead kittens in her poetry.
The way her cackling shoulder shrieks, when goosebumps form
with delight.

It's almost camouflaged,
the way she hides her breasts behind layers of clothes.
As if to imply they weren't a part of her,
underneath her blouse.
As if ashamed to be seen or touched.

It's almost biblical,
the way she poisoned me with her laughter of near sanity.
The way she polishes her smile to resemble that of happiness.
And the way the kiss in her stare, bears resemblance to Judas.

It's almost tragic,
that when she's killing me, my love for her increases.
And while she's piling on the circumstances in this game called
love,
all I can think about is

                                        -she's like a baseball and
I'm just pitching her around the field.

Crystal Rain (A Lyric)

Verse: 1
The moon cried me a river
That rippled in the dark
And all I saw was an angel
Standing by my windowpane
She glanced at me for a moment
With a kind of iridescent spark
That filled my heart with warmth inside the rain
I tried to get her attention
And I tried to know her name
But she kept walking
And she kept talking

Inside the crystal rain

Chorus:
There was a poverty
Within my eyes
As I longed to grasp her hand
It kept me hidden inside
My bottled-up shell of pain
I ran outside to find her
In lightning and in thunder
But no remnants of her
Had yet left an earthly stain

As she was lost inside
The blackened crystal rain
And I longed to know
The words that formed her name

Verse: 2
The thunder quickly subsided
And the moonlight then provided
A pattern within the ruins of the rain
And with everything within me
With sheer bitterness and envy
I felt an emptiness in me
That filled my heart and brain
Because I lost the spark
Inside the crystal rain
And because I'd never find
The meaning behind the name

Chorus:
There was a poverty
Within my eyes
As I longed to grasp her hand
It kept me hidden inside
My bottled-up shell of pain
I ran outside to find her
In lightning and in thunder
But no remnants of her
Had yet left an earthly stain

As she was lost inside
The blackened crystal rain
And I longed to know
The words that formed her name

Verse 3:
But then the night was quickly fading
And I had stopped debating
Whether or not I'd find my maiden

In my shadowed stench of shame
I fell to my knees in sorrow
And looked up to find my tomorrow
Shaped like a silhouetted sun in shadow
That eliminated all my pain
And I saw her on the crystal dawn
As she spelled out her name
And I never again
Clouded myself with blame
Because I now knew the meaning

Behind the crystal rain

Paradox

A fish born in the desert
A cactus born at sea
A man born on the moon
No life inside of me

A tree with no roots
A cat without lives
Earth with no gravity
A life without surprise